Reverdy Johnson

A further consideration of the dangerous condition of the country

Reverdy Johnson

A further consideration of the dangerous condition of the country

ISBN/EAN: 9783337235260

Printed in Europe, USA, Canada, Australia, Japan

Cover: Foto ©Andreas Hilbeck / pixelio.de

More available books at **www.hansebooks.com**

A FURTHER CONSIDERATION

OF

THE DANGEROUS

Condition of the Country,

THE

CAUSES WHICH HAVE LED TO IT.

And the Duty of the People.

BY A MARYLANDER.

BALTIMORE:
THE SUN JOB PRINTING ESTABLISHMENT.
1867.

The writer's reasons for the publication of this pamphlet are stated in its commencement. The labor of preparing it and the one of last month, (if it had not been, as it was, a labor of duty,) will be fully compensated, if they shall be found to contribute in any degree to correct in the public mind the Constitutional errors he has endeavored to expose, and to cause the people of the country to come to the rescue of our institutions from the dangers in which they are involved, and to the relief of our Southern brethren and their restoration to every Constitutional right.

REVERDY JOHNSON.

Baltimore, November 15th, 1867.

The Condition of the Country.

In the pamphlet entitled "The Dangerous Condition of the Country," &c., issued during the last month, the writer, amongst other things, discussed the meaning of the clause in the Constitution of the general Government which provides that "the United States shall guarantee to every State in this Union a republican form of government." At the request of friends in Maryland and in other States, he proposes to pursue that inquiry further, and also to expose what he believes to be perilous errors in relation to other clauses of the Constitution.

I. The meaning of the clause of guarantee. It is obvious that the statesmen of '89 considered the several State governments, then existing, as republican in form. Their purpose therefore, was to secure to each State a government of like form with that which each possessed at that time. Upon any other construction of the clause it would have been the duty of the first Congress assembled under the Constitution to have provided for such a change in the government of each State as would, according to their view, have made it republican. This was not done, nor was the idea of its necessity suggested until within the last year or two. The fact of this long and settled acquiescence of Congress and of the people of the country in the opinion of our Fathers, that the State governments were republican, should be held conclusive upon the point. Any other view would charge the members of the first Congress, (most of whom were members of the convention which framed the Constitution,) and of each succeeding one, with gross ignorance, or a flagrant dereliction of duty. It would, also, impute to the people the singular error of not understanding the nature of their own State governments. The guarantee deals exclusively with the form of government, and not with the powers conferred upon it. After the Declaration of Independence, and down to the adoption of the Constitution, each of the State governments was sovereign, and possessed all the powers which its people might endow it with. This sovereignty and scope of authority are now limited only by the powers conferred upon the general Government, and the restrictions imposed upon the States. Over their merely internal concerns their jurisdiction is as paramount as it was before the Constitution was adopted. As has been well said, theirs is a " domestic sovereignty " as contradistinguished from that external sovereignty which belongs to the general Government. That the regulation of the elective franchise was in the States before '89 will be admitted. That it was not the design of the Constitution to take it away, or to limit it, is perfectly clear ; first, because Congress has no powers except such as are delegated, and this is not delegated ; and, second, because the power is expressly recognised as a continuing one in the States, in the second section of the first article, which provides that in the choice of members of the House of Representatives by the people of the States the electors " shall have the qualifications requisite for electors of the most numerous branch of the State Legislature." Thus there is not only no authority given to Congress to regulate the franchise, but a clear inhibition of it by the express adoption of the State regulations. Can it be doubted that the men of '89, who had but recently emerged triumphantly from a war to establish republican liberty, would have failed to have remodeled their State governments so as to make them republican in form, if they had thought they were not so already? The history of that struggle and their subsequent conduct shews that they abjured monarchical and aristocratic governments as, in their judgment, fatal to freedom. Will any reasonable man question that, in the opinion of its framers and of the people who ratified it, the Constitution of the United

States creates a government republican in form? To do so would be to impute hypocrisy to both, for, they all not only professed to admire that form, but almost to detest every other, being of opinion that that, and that only, could secure the liberty to acquire which they had, for a period of seven years, poured out their treasure and their blood. This being so, then, in the judgment of our forefathers that government is in form republican. And yet, as has been shewn, it possesses no power over the elective franchise. On the contrary, it leaves that to be regulated by governments subordinate to itself—the States. It also makes one branch of its legislature to consist of a territorial representation, without regard to the extent of each territory or the population belonging to it. The smallest of the original States in limits and population, Rhode Island and Delaware, were given an equal voice with New York and Pennsylvania in that branch, the Senate. And this provision was made to apply to every State which might thereafter be admitted into the Union, and was deemed so vital to the continuing existence of the Union that it was placed beyond the power of the people to change it without the consent of the State to be affected, the Constitution providing "that no State, without its consent, shall be deprived of its equal suffrage in the Senate."—*Art. V.*

It is obvious, therefore, that the wise and patriotic men of those days considered the unrestricted powers of the States over the elective franchise to be perfectly consistent with a republican form of government, and that even the absence of any authority over it in the general Government, and the leaving Federal elections to be held according to State regulations were also perfectly consistent with the idea that the Government of the Union is republican. That they did not hold universal suffrage or equality of representation to be a necessary element in that form of government, is plain from their giving equal representation of the States in the Senate, and from the provision that each State shall have an equal voice in the choice of a President when the electoral colleges fail to elect. (Art. 2, sect. 1.) How can a sane man imagine that the Government of the United States is not republican, and was not deemed to be so by its authors? If this is not clear from what has been already said, it will be so from the further view that the only security the States have, not within themselves, of continuing to enjoy republican governments, is in the clause of guarantee, for, can it be conceived that that only security would be entrusted to a government not itself republican? There never lived men better fitted to establish republican governments, and to provide for their perpetuity, than the men of our revolutionary period. The usurpations of the mother country, utterly incompatible with the freedom of the colonies, necessarily turned their thoughts to political studies. The science of government was the subject of their meditation by day and by night. They were perfectly familiar with the republics of Rome, Sparta and Athens, and all the governments of the past, and knew their faults and their virtues. They saw in those republics the dangers of an unrestrained, tumultuous democracy. They also saw how unfit for our condition were governments monarchical or aristocratic, and resolved to avoid the perils incident to them all. They determined to maintain their then well regulated State governments, which in their opinion, as is historically obvious, were republican, and to secure their perpetuity, by giving to the general Government—which they thought, as is equally plain, was also republican—the power and the ability to accomplish it.

With this understanding of the term by the men who framed the Constitution, it would violate its legal meaning to give it a different interpretation. It is a rule of construction applicable to every written instrument that its terms are to be understood, according to the intent of its framers, and this rule for very obvious reasons is especially applicable to a written Constitution. A different one would not only defeat the intent of its authors, but would cause the interpretation to be as changeable as the varying opinions of the hour. It would be one thing to-day, and another to-morrow. In regard to the term in question, the State governments would be now republican, and, now anti-republican,—and thus, what was designed to be a fixed

and well defined term, would ve as shifting as the clouds. A
result so absurd, so inconsistent with the object of a constitution, demonstrates its unsound ess. The necessary and only
safe principle is at all times to give to the terms used in such an
instrument their intended meaning. If that meaning, in the
case of a constitution, is thought by the people to be dangerous
to their rights or injurious to their interest, they are not without
remedy, for they can avert either difficulty by changing the
constitution. The idea that universal suffrage is absolutely
necessary to republican government, rests upon the assumption
that the right to vote is inherent in man's nature and as
inalienable as is his right to life or liberty, and, upon the further
assumption that to deprive him of it virtually makes him a
political slave. Both assumptions are altogether unwarranted ;
first, because no government ever existed in which universal
suffrage prevailed, and, as every school-boy knows, there have
been governments of the republican form ; secondly, because
freedom does not depend upon the rights of franchise, for if it
did, then, in this country eve male person under the age of
twenty-one, and every female of any age, and every alien who
has not consummated his naturalization, would not be free.
The whole theory as to the right is erroneous ; it has no natural
foundation whatever, but is the creature of positive law, and
has been so considered from th beginning of the world's civilization to the present time by every writer on governments, and
has been so treated by every government that history records.
It has been made to depend upon sex, citizenship, age, residence, and other circumstances. and such regulations have been
different in different governments. No one until recently has
denied that each government has the sole power to make and
modify regulations of the kind at will, unlike the rights of life
and liberty of which a man cannot be justly deprived, if he has
committed no crime. It is for the people of every State to
decide for themselves who among them shall be entitled to the
elective franchise. When a majority makes that decision by a
constitution of government, all are bound by it, and no one can
claim the right except those to whom it is granted. And this

has been the uniform doctrine upon the subject. The world, therefore, has been in error, and our fathers have shared in that error, if, as the political sciolists of our times maintain, this right is the same as that of life and liberty. But if their doctrine was correct, (instead of being pestilentially heretical,) it would follow that the right *to be voted for* is equally inherent and inalienable. And, yet, to this extent they do not at present go. The qualifications to hold office, in every republican government of which we have any knowledge, are different and higher than those required of the voter. Greater age, a longer residence, and a higher property qualification, where such a qualification is to be possessed by the voter, have almost always been provided for. And no one in these days has ventured even to insinuate that provisions of this kind are incompatible with the nature of such a government, or violate any of the rights of man.

II. The writer has very recently been informed that another ground than that of limited suffrage is relied upon by some of the members of Congress, known as radicals, to prove that the government of Maryland is not republican. It is because of the alleged unequal apportionment of representation in its legislature. This, if possible, is more unfounded than the other. It has never before been doubted that it was for the people of each State to decide, without the interposition of the general Government, how their State shall be divided, both as regards territory and population, in reference to representation in its legislature. And to what extent there should be a territorial representation in that department, without regard to population, and a representation dependent upon population were matters, also, heretofore conceded to be within their sole power. In Maryland, by her Constitution of '76, there was in part a territorial representation in the Senate, and a popular one in the House of Delegates, but in regard to neither was there equality. On the contrary, in relation to representation in the House, there was great inequality. That Constitution was framed by some of the wisest and most patriotic republicans known to history. They never conceived that this inequality affected the republican nature of the government, or to any extent assimilated it to any other. In this happy ignorance, as our modern wiseacres would have it, they continued contentedly for very many years, and until the most, if not all of them, had descended into honored graves, leaving behind them names which their posterity will ever gratefully cherish and be proud of. At each subsequent change of our State government these inequalities have been found. The counties into which the State was divided, although they differed greatly in size and in population, were each of them entitled to one Senator in the Senate of the State, whilst in the other House the representation was not made to conform to anything like equality of population, and, during all this time, the people of the State and of the country in their simplicity believed that her government was republican. But if the test of equal representation as to population is admitted, what would be its practical operation? The population of a State, in its several divisions of counties or districts, varies from year to year, from month to month. To-day it may be the same in each ; to-morrow not ; to-day, according to this test, the government would be republican, to-morrow anti-republican ; so that the form of government which is to be judged of by its Constitution would not be fixed and immutable, but as changeable as the tides of population. This ineffable absurdity proves the inadmissibility of the test.

There has been, however, a Congressional Committee in session for a few months past inquiring whether the Government of Maryland is republican. Of the many witnesses they are said to have examined, all are of that very small party in the State known as Radical. That party was in power under the Constitution of '64, declared by competent authority to have been legally adopted. A decided majority of the domestic vote was against it. It was carried, however, by a small majority, by the vote of the soldiers, most of whom, as was believed, were not legal voters. By that Constitution the franchise was limited to white men, and of these a large majority were excluded by restrictions, in their nature unjust and punitive. Under that Constitution a very small minority of her people controlled the government of the State. And yet, notwithstanding the exclusion from the franchise of the blacks, and a large portion of the whites, the very parties who are seeking through Congress the destruction of our present government, never pretended that that of '64 was not republican. Strange inconsistency! Unsurpassed effrontery! A minority government is republican! A majority one is not! The exclusion of the negroes and of the whites from the franchise in 1864 in no manner impeached the republican character of that Constitution, whilst the same exclusion of the blacks and the enfranchisement of the whites—who, as is proved by the election of the fifth of this month, constitute a large majority of all the male adults of the State, white and black—shews that our Government under the Constitution of 1867 is anti-republican! Not only does the recent election prove that a large majority of all the male adults in Maryland, black and white, support her government, but that every county and the city of Baltimore have sent to the Legislature representatives of the same opinion. The majority for the Governor of the State, just elected, is without previous precedent in her history, being 41,712, (*forty-one thousand seven hundred and twelve.*) That election establishes another important fact—that the people of the State are now more dissatisfied with radical men and measures, than they were when they ratified their present Constitution, the majority in favor of that having been 24,124, whilst the one just stated was nearly twice as great. How strange is it then that there should be a committee appointed by the House of Representatives sitting in secret (for they refused to permit a representative of the State to be present, although he demanded it as a right, as he justly could) and endeavoring, through the testimony of the men who framed and held office under the Constitution of 1864, to prove that the present Constitution is not republican. How absurd is it, too, in such an inquiry to examine witnesses. The form of a Government, its nature and character, when created by a written Constitution, must depend upon the Constitution itself. If this is not republican no oral testimony can make it so ; and if it is republican, no such testimony can make it otherwise. It is reported, and the writer believes correctly,that the committee have inquired of witnesses,whether a particular appropriation of money was recently made by the municipal authorities of Baltimore to be used in preventing some anticipated legislation by the State, and in what manner was it used. What tendency such facts can have towards proving the character of the State Government, passes all reasonable comprehension.

III. Has it ever been contended before, that under the guarantee clause, Congress has a right to make a Constitution for a State? And yet this is virtually what is now attempted in regard to Maryland, Delaware and Kentucky.

If they can do this they have the power to decide when and how to do it. A startling pretension, certainly ! If there be any right ever held dear by the people of this country, it is that of forming their own State governments. But how is the power, if it exists, to be exerted ? Is Congress of itself to frame a Constitution and force it upon a State, not only without regard to, but against the known will of her people ? And is this to be done in the name and on behalf of republican Freedom ? Can any measure be more antagonistic to the idea of such Freedom ? And if Congress is not to do the work itself, but to leave it to the people of the State, it can only accomplish the end by reserving the right to reject such a Constitution, as in the case of one framed by the people of a territory. What then is to be the condition of States which insist upon a Constitution which is objectionable to Congress? They will be without a Constitution, or have one forced upon them by Congress which that body may approve. And what is the character of the force to be exerted? It must be physical, not moral, military, not civil—which is State destruction. This is not making the military subordinate to the civil authority, as the security of liberty requires, but paramount. It is, in fact, to give to Congress the power to establish military governments in every one of the States ; to subject the people of each, not to the mild influence of wise and humane laws, but

14

to the power of any military man whom Congress shall see proper
to place over them, as Congress has done in relation to ten
of the States of the Union. The result of this experiment
has not been such as to commend it to the good sense
and patriotic feeling of a free people.

Mr. Stevens, of Pa., the very head and front of the radical
portion of the republican party in the House of Representatives,
in a recent letter to a German professor, (who, by the by, with
wretched taste, says that our fathers failed to approach near " to
the true principles of liberty," and that there is in the Constitu-
ion a "great blot" and " heinous crime"—a gross libel upon our
most illustrious dead,) maintains that, since what he errone-
ously says has taken place, (the adoption of the 14th amendment) he has no doubt of the power of Congress " to regulate
the elective franchise, so far as it regards the whole nation, in
every State of the Union." The amendment confers no such
power. It only provides : 1. That persons born in the United
States, or naturalized and subject to its jurisdiction, are
citizens thereof, and of the State of their residence. 2. That
no State shall make or enforce any law which shall abridge the
privileges and immunities of citizens of the United States.
3. That no person shall be deprived of life, liberty, or property
without due process of law, or be denied equal protection of the
laws. There is nothing in either of these provisions from which
the power in question can be implied. Under the Constitution,
independent of this supposed amendment, the provisions as to
the rights of citizens are the same as those of the amendment.
And yet Mr. Stevens himself admits, what no one has until
lately denied, that Congress had no authority to interfere with
suffrage in the States. How then can the amendment be held
to confer that authority ? I have said that in relation to this
subject the Constitution and the amendment are the same. Are
they not? Will Mr. Stevens, or any other man of sense, maintain that under the Constitution, without the amendment, a
State could, by law, " abridge the privileges and immunities
of citizens," or deprive any person " of life, liberty or property
without due process of law." And these are all that the

amendment prohibits. The fact is, that the provisions just referred to are wholly unnecessary. If the amendment had contained but the single clause defining citizenship, the Constitution would have supplied all of the securities enumerated in the second and third clauses. If, therefore, as Mr. Stevens concedes, citizenship does not confer the right to vote, or give to Congress any power to confer it upon the citizen, the amendment gives neither the right nor the power. Indeed, to construe the clause otherwise would make it the duty of Congress to secure the franchise to every citizen, irrespective of age, residence, sex or color. For, if it be a right incident to citizenship, Congress has not only no power to deny or abridge it, but, on the contrary, is bound to protect it. The fact is, that Mr. Stevens' interpretation of the amendment is an entire misapprehension of its meaning and purpose. The original Constitution does not define citizenship, and different opinions upon the point having been entertained, the object of the amendment was merely to supply that omission, as it does by declaring that birth and naturalization shall give it. And, as it had been held by the Supreme Court, in the Dred Scott decision, that the descendant of an African, born within the United States, was not a citizen, the language of the first clause was designedly made so comprehensive as to include that class. In fact, the design was to provide that the same circumstances (birth or naturalization) shall make a black as well as a white man a citizen. It seems to me, then, perfectly plain that the exclusive right of the States to regulate suffrage, admitted by Mr. Stevens to belong to them prior to the amendment, belongs to them still. This must be so, unless citizenship in the United States of itself gives the right to vote—a proposition too extravagant to be believed in by any but a perverted understanding.

Upon the whole subject of the guarantee clause it is submitted: 1. That its meaning is entirely different from that which the radicals of the day impute to it. 2. That the existing governments of the States are and have always been republican in form. 3. That the sole office of the clause is to secure to them that form. 4. That the opposite construction would, in practice, be destructive of the rights of the States and of the people. 5. That such a construction is repudiated by the entire past history of our country. And, lastly, that there is nothing in the supposed 14th amendment which in any way enlarges the power of Congress in this respect. In what I have thus far said of the amendment, I have assumed that it has been constitutionally ratified. But this is certainly not the fact, unless the ten Southern States are not States of the Union. In my former pamphlet I quoted a recent decision of Chief Justice Chase, to shew that, in the judgment of the judicial department of the Government, their character as such States was not lost by the rebellion. His language is, that the rebellion did not "EFFECT, EVEN FOR A MOMENT, THE SEPARATION OF NORTH CAROLINA FROM THE UNION."

The contrary hypothesis goes upon the assumption that the late civil war extinguished them as such States, and gave to the United States the same title to the territory embraced within their boundaries, and the same authority over their people, as if they had been conquered from a foreign enemy. A word or two more upon this point. If this be true it would follow that the United States could transfer them and their people to another nation, for what is obtained by conquest, and has not afterwards become a State of the Union, the Government of the Union can cede away. And, yet, so far, no one has been reckless enough to say that such a cession can be constitutionally made of these States. In truth, such an act would be a cession by the Government of a vital portion of itself. These States not having in the words of the Chief Justice "even for a moment" lost their character or connection with the Union as States, the amendment in question has not been ratified so as to make it a part of the Constitution.

IV. The impeachment power. Upon this point the writer thinks that very erroneous and mischievous doctrines are held by some of our public men. These errors are: 1. As to what may be the subject of the power. 2. As to what Congress can do pending the trial. The provisions of the Constitution are, in regard to the first: that the impeachment is to be for "treason, bribery or other high crimes and misdemeanors;" and upon the second: that when the President is impeached (and to that case the writer will confine himself) the trial shall be by the Senate, and that two-thirds of the members present shall be necessary to a conviction, and that the judgment is not to extend "further than to removal from office and disqualification to hold and enjoy any office of honor, trust or profit under the United States." 1. From the beginning of the Government it has been uniformly decided by the Supreme Court that there are no common law offences prohibited by the Constitution except such as are specially named. In the clause before us the only offences so designated are treason and bribery. For the nature of these offences the courts have a right to refer to the common law for their definition. But it is otherwise as to the general terms high crimes and misdemeanors. These not being specified, and there being no common law jurisdiction in the courts of the Union, they can not take cognizance of them without statutory authority. If this was not so, the doctrine of the judiciary would be palpably wrong. But if it be wrong—if there may, under this clause, be a crime and misdemeanor not made so by statute—this is certain, that there must be some law making it so. No act, therefore, which the President may do is cause of impeachment unless it be treason or bribery, or declared criminal by statute or the common law. Any other construction would place it in the power of the House of Representatives to make any act of the President, though not prohibited by law and wholly innocent, a crime and misdemeanor, which would be to place the President in absolute dependence upon Congress, contrary to the obvious design of the Constitution. The result is, that the President can only be impeached for treason or bribery or for some act made by statute a high crime and misdemeanor. Any alleged violation of a supposed duty, not made a crime by statute, any alleged violation of party fealty, any use of his official patronage which politicians may find fault with, or which may have proved injurious to the public interest, are not causes of impeachment.

2.—What power has Congress during the trial? It is contended, and, as the writer believes, for the first time, that by statute the President may be suspended from all the functions of his office. Clearly, this power is not in terms given by the Constitution. On the contrary, by its very words he is to remain in office until he shall have been constitutionally convicted—a conviction which can only be had upon the vote of two-thirds of the Senators present. If the convention had designed to give to Congress the power in question, is it conceivable that they would not have done so in plain terms? If they had deemed such a suspension to be necessary to the public good, would they have left it to depend entirely upon the discretion of Congress? Or would they not, as in the case of his permanent removal, have made it the subject of Constitutional provision? But we are not left, however, to mere argument upon the subject. The power, it was suggested by a member of the convention, should be delegated to Congress. The suggestion met with no favor—it was generally repudiated. Amongst others, Mr. Madison opposed it upon the ground that it would enable a mere majority of each House to effect the temporary removal of a President who might prove obnoxious to them, and to take to themselves the benefit of all the patronage of the office, by placing in it some person who would dispose of such patronage to their advantage. (It will not be deemed extravagant or unjust to add, that the foresight of Mr. Madison is illustrated by what, it is said, is now contemplated by some of the leading men of the radical branch of the republican party.) But the doctrine is not only without warrant in the Constitution, but is repugnant to its obvious purpose.

The whole executive power is vested in the President, and he holds it subject only to removal when convicted on impeachment, and, with that exception, not under, but against any power conferred upon Congress. In many respects it is given to him to check the inconsiderate or unconstitutional acts of that body. He is to be elected by electors chosen by the people, and no authority is given to Congress in regard to the election, except in the contingency of the failure of the electors to elect. The House of Representatives has no control over him except by impeachment, and the Senate can only convict upon the judgment of two-thirds of its members. His power to arrest the legislation of Congress by veto, can not be overruled, except by two-thirds of each House. It is evident from these several provisions that it was not the design to subject him or his powers to the authority of a mere majority of the legislature. The practical result of a power to suspend might be to work his removal. The House impeaches, and the majority of that body and of the Senate suspends during the trial : two-thirds of the latter branch cannot be brought to convict ; the House again impeaches and suspension is again provided for ; and the same proceeding may be resorted to, on every successive failure in the Senate to convict, until his term of office expires. During the whole period the executive power of the Government is to be wielded by a man, not selected by the people, but by a bare majority of each House. Can it be imagined that such results as these were contemplated by the Convention? If it cannot, it is submitted that the power has no place in the Constitution. The writer, therefore, maintains that there can be no impeachment except for treason or bribery, or for some act which by statute has been made a high crime and misdemeanor.

V. The settled opinion of this country (justified by all history) has ever been, that political liberty and individual rights, can be best secured by a written Constitution, limiting and defining the powers of the Government. Unrestricted power, whether vested in one or in many, is always dangerous. It is but the power of the despot, fatal alike to social and private rights and interests. It is, therefore, all important that the public mind shall adhere to the opinions upon this subject, which our fathers firmly and devotedly held. Until very recently, the considerate men of the country, were becoming apprehensive, that a majority of our people were about to abandon these principles. The result of the elections during this and the preceding month has cheered them with a hope that such will not be the case. The voice which these elections

.ve uttered is so commanding, that, if it does not fail to arrest
e course of the present Congress, and force them to adopt a
nservative and Constitutional policy, it will soon call into
wer a different set of servants. The writer, for himself, has
t fully shared in those apprehensions. He has always felt a
nviction, that the assaults upon the Constitution—the viola-
n of its most sacred provisions—and the distracted and dis-
essed condition to which the country would be brought by
em, would at an early day awaken the patriotism and love
freedom, which he believes are too deeply seated in the
arts of the people ever to be eradicated. That the Constitu-
n has not been and is not now observed by the dominant
rty in Congress, he thinks he has demonstrated.

That the condition of the country is a distressing one all
ust admit. Who has read a recent address of a convention
' the white citizens of South Carolina without sympathy and
in? The sad state of their section they describe with a
uching eloquence, power, and truth, which must excite admi-
tion and awaken solicitude. They have made their appeal,
t in a pusillanimous, but in a manly and patriotic spirit.
hey invoke the justice and humanity of their race—express
> hostility to the rightful authority of the United States
-admit that the doctrine of secession can no longer be
aintained, and that the institution of slavery is terminated
rever. In their own words, " slavery is at an end," and they
isclaim any purpose or wish to reinstate it. What they ask
, to be permitted to participate, equally with the Northern men
' their race, in the privileges and securities of a common gov-
nment. They, above all, implore such brethren not to subject
em to the dominion of an ignorant African race, just emerged
om slavery, uneducated, devoid of all knowledge of the
rinciples upon which rest our free institutions, and who can
nly become the instruments of bad and designing men. What
icy want, is peace, benign peace, which carries with it security
id happiness,—not the peace which reigns in the home-
.ead whose inmates have been butchered by a savage foe, not
ie peace of the Desert—but peace guarded and protected

by civil laws, such as freemen have a right to demand.— Disclaiming any "factious opposition to the reconstruction acts of Congress," they tell us for what they desire peace; that it is to enable them to build upon waste places "our temples of worship, our sacked and ruined cities now lying in ashes, our dismantled dwellings and our prostrate credit, for its holy christian influence, and for the civilization and refinement which spring up in its path." Shall this appeal be in vain? Forbid it, justice! Forbid it humanity! Forbid it, our common origin, our past and equal renown as defenders of the rights and honor of our nation upon the ocean and the land, and as equal contributors, in the public councils, to the safety, prosperity and happiness of the whole country! But, the writer has no fear that the appeal will be in vain. For it is, now, the demonstrated determination of the white men of the North, the East, the West, and the far Pacific, to have the Constitution respected, and to continue the governments, State and national, exclusively in the hands of men of their own race. When this is done, the South will soon be restored to former prosperity— will be once more a storehouse largely contributing to the wealth and happiness of the nation—and be, as in the past, the abode of the intelligent and refined, dispensing an elegant hospitality, which has ever been proverbial. And then, better than all, her people and those of the other States will be bound together by ties far stronger than any that Constitutions can create—the ties of mutual interest and affection.

A MARYLANDER.

www.ingramcontent.com/pod-product-compliance
Lightning Source LLC
Chambersburg PA
CBHW021610270326
41931CB00009B/1419